A HISTORY OF FASHION

FOR CHILDREN

CELIA JOICEY AND
DENNIS NOTHDRUFT

A History of Fashion

FOR CHILDREN

ILLUSTRATED BY Rose Blake

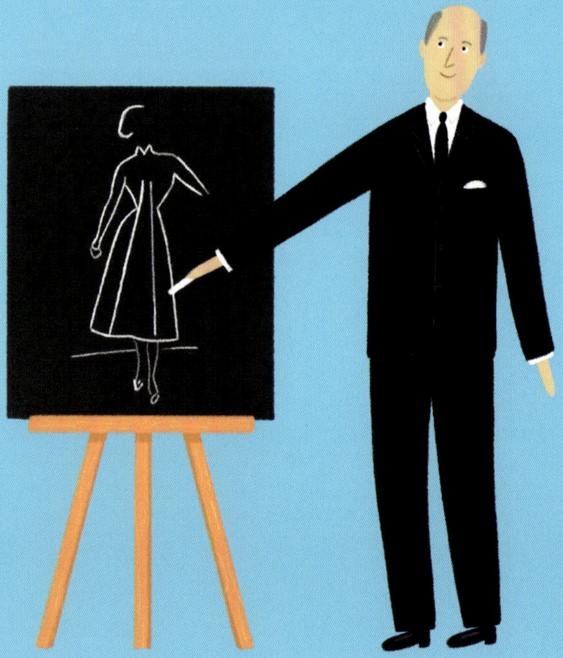

CONTENTS

6   INTRODUCTION

8   **Chapter 1: WHAT IS FASHION?**
Why do we care about what we wear?

18   **Chapter 2: DRESSING UP**
How have clothes changed through time?

32   **Chapter 3: THE FASHION REVOLUTION**
Fashion from 1650 to 1900

46   **Chapter 4: CLOTHES FOR A MODERN WORLD**
Fashion from 1900 to the present

70   **Chapter 5: THE FASHION INDUSTRY**
Makers, materials, models, and more . . .

88   Timeline of Inventions
92   Glossary
94   List of Illustrations
95   Index

INTRODUCTION

What are you wearing today? We humans have been putting clothes on our bodies for the whole of recorded history. Some traditional types of clothing have been worn for centuries, like the kimono in Japan, and the sari in India. Other garments have changed quite dramatically as society has developed. This changeable way of dressing is what we call "fashion" and it is the subject of our book.

Radical changes in clothing through the centuries tell a fascinating story of different peoples, cultures, and times. You can pick a style to express yourself and—though you may not know it—you will also be reflecting the society and time that you live in.

I'm Celia and I'm one of the authors of this book. I work in a gallery that showcases art, fashion, and design. I believe clothes can change the way you feel.

My name is Dennis and I work at the Fashion and Textile Museum in London, where I organize exhibitions. Today I am wearing my favorite Japanese designs.

In these pages, we'll explore how fashion influences what we wear, how we feel about ourselves, and—significantly—how we look! Fashion affects everyone. Even the kimono and sari have changed as people's tastes have altered, and new textiles have been invented. In the past, fashionable clothing was mostly for the rich, but today—thanks to innovations like the sewing machine—many more people can afford to wear it. This book will show you how the way we dress is influenced by where we shop and what pictures we see in the media.

Our illustrator Rose Blake and Choupette the cat will join you on this journey through time to discover talented fashion designers, famously flamboyant outfits, funny footwear, and much more. Dip in and out as you wish. The timeline on page 88 will guide you through some important dates and inventions, and the glossary on page 92 will help with any words you might not know. So, stay cool or dress warm, and settle in. It's time to focus on fashion!

I'm Rose and I'm the illustrator of this book. My artwork is full of bright colors and bold patterns, and so is my closet!

My name is Choupette and I am the cat of famous fashion designer Karl Lagerfeld. I like to time travel and take inspiration from history.

WHAT IS FASHION?
Why do we care about what we wear?

I'm Jean Paul Gaultier and I'm a French fashion designer. I like to shake things up in my designs—mixing different styles, and challenging traditional ideas about gender.

I'm Frida Kahlo and I'm an artist from Mexico. I care about what I wear because I want to stand out from the crowd. To celebrate my heritage, I like to wear traditional Mexican dress.

I'm King Henry VIII. I wear clothes that make me look huge and important, and I like expensive and fashionable materials like velvet and silk. I care about what I wear because I want everybody to know that I'm a king.

1. What is fashion?

Identity

Who are you? How you dress can help you to define your place in the world. Does your country have a national costume or traditional dress? Even if you only wear it for a special occasion, such clothing can play an important role in how you identify with your heritage and with others. Traditional forms of dress are timeless, and therefore never go out of fashion.

In contrast, fashionable clothes and accessories keep changing with time. They often reflect the unwritten rules of the society they are worn in. For example, in 19th-century Europe, men were expected to wear pants, while women always wore dresses or skirts. Likewise, the color black became associated with funeral dress and white with weddings.

1. What is fashion?

In the 20th century, expectations around what to wear were challenged again and again, as Western society's rules changed. In the 1920s, women began to wear pants. Then in the 1980s, fashion designers such as *Jean Paul Gaultier* (b. 1952) created skirts for men, questioning what menswear could be.

Today, people use fashion to express not only the identity of the society or group they belong to, but also their own personal identity. There are far fewer rules and the choices of what to wear are almost endless. The way you dress can be an opportunity to show your values and beliefs, or simply how you feel on the day.

Social status

Are you a prince or a pauper, or somewhere in between? Throughout history, people have cared what their clothes say about their social position. In ancient Greece, the color purple—made from the most expensive dye—expressed nobility. In 10th-century Japan, women at the imperial court wore the jūnihitoe, which had twelve or more layers, as a symbol of their high status. Jewelry and luxury fabrics such as silk have also been used to show off a person's wealth and importance.

This 18th-century woodblock print depicts the Japanese poet Ono no Komachi (c. 825–900), dressed in formal jūnihitoe.

In Europe, from the Middle Ages onward, the growth of trade transformed many people's experience of clothing. As ordinary people grew richer, they were able to afford luxury goods. Medieval rulers did not like this! So, they introduced hundreds of rules—called sumptuary laws—to set themselves apart from the lower classes. In England, the "Acts of Apparel" dictated in great detail what clothing people from different social classes were allowed to wear. Only royals, for example, could wear purple silk or gold cloth.

1. What is fashion?

For centuries in Europe, dress was also influenced by the power and wealth of the Christian church. In medieval Italy, vanity and extravagance were thought of as sinful. One sumptuary law even dictated how many rings a woman could wear on each hand. In contrast, English *King Henry VIII* (1491–1547) used his expensive clothing to highlight his perceived closeness to God. As the head of the Church of England, his wide-shouldered doublets, crimson fabrics, gold embroidery, and bejeweled capes reinforced his claim of divine right to be on the throne.

The term "conspicuous consumption" was coined in the 20th century to describe the purchase of clothing and other goods specifically to display the buyer's wealth. However, it is more difficult today to spot a person's wealth just from the style of their dress. If you want to highlight your wealth and status through clothing nowadays, you usually have to wear expensive materials, as well as designer brands.

1. What is fashion?

Beauty

Do you adore to be adorned? Humans have always sought to make themselves more attractive based on their society's beauty ideals. In the earliest times, body paint, and found materials, such as feathers or plants, were used for decoration. As technology and human ingenuity advanced, new techniques and materials were developed to decorate the body: weaving and knitting for cloth, and metal and clay for jewelry.

Many ways have been devized to embellish clothing. In medieval Europe, buttons were an expensive luxury, often made in gold or silver, or decorated with jewels. You could show off your wealth by wearing fashions with many buttons—this was the most stylish way to both decorate and fasten your clothes in 14th-century France.

In Papua New Guinea, members of different tribes gather together every year for sing-sing festivals, where they wear traditional dress and paint their bodies to perform ancestral dances and songs and share their cultural traditions.

In modern times, we enjoy a wide range of fastenings to bind our garments. Do any of the items you're wearing today have buttons, buckles, belts, ties, zips, snaps, or Velcro?

Fashionable accessories have always been popular. From the 17th century onward, people liked to wear fancy gloves to display their wealth. Then the 18th century was known as the golden age of the fan. These could be decorated with beautiful pictures, or you could use them to flash a secret message to an admirer. In the 19th century, men liked to carry fine walking sticks. In modern fashion, we still have many accessories to choose from—shoes, socks, hats, scarves, sunglasses, jewelry . . . the list goes on.

1. What is fashion?

Individuality

Be yourself! Certain people throughout history are remembered as much for their individual sense of style as for their actions. Here are a few famous figures who have used their clothing to distinguish themselves from the people around them. In turn, they have set fashion trends that others have followed.

Elizabeth I of England (1533–1603)
Queen Elizabeth I was one of the most famous women in Western history, ruling England for forty-five years. She used her clothing to show her wealth and power, often draping herself in ropes of pearls and expensive lace. The queen's elaborate dresses gave her the appearance of a goddess or a statue.

Oscar Wilde (1854–1900)
Oscar Wilde was an Irish writer and celebrity, known for his witty sayings and his plays. He was also noted for his extravagant dress sense, which featured green carnations, velvet knickerbocker suits, sweeping capes, and large brimmed hats worn at a jaunty angle. Wilde chose his clothing to express his sense of beauty and to shock his stuffy fellow Victorians.

Frida Kahlo (1907–1954)
Artist Frida Kahlo chose to express her cultural identity by wearing the traditional dress of Indigenous women from her home country of Mexico. She painted many self-portraits and her distinctive style gained attention worldwide. Her example continues to inspire people today to express themselves as a work of art.

Prince (1958–2016)
American musician and singer Prince developed a flamboyant style both on stage and off. His love of diamonds and pearls, and shirts with frills was considered controversial at the time. However, many people soon started to copy his style, right down to his signature preference for the color purple.

Rihanna (b. 1988)
Musician, actress, and business owner Rihanna is known for her bold and innovative style choices. Her ability to effortlessly blend streetwear with high fashion has made her a style icon and trendsetter. From the red carpet to everyday looks, she often experiments with bold colors, unexpected shapes and textures, and eye-catching accessories.

1. What is fashion?

17

2

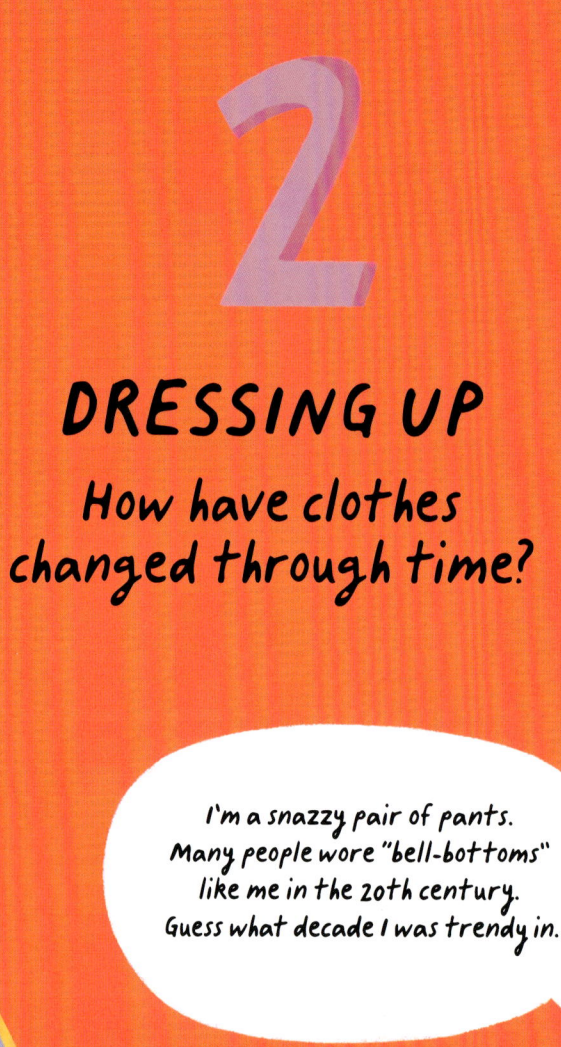

DRESSING UP

How have clothes changed through time?

I'm a snazzy pair of pants. Many people wore "bell-bottoms" like me in the 20th century. Guess what decade I was trendy in.

I'm a fancy top hat. People still wear me for special occasions, but when I was popular in the 19th century, I was often worn everyday.

I'm a very ancient boat-shaped shoe. Can you guess what country I was worn in?

2. Dressing up

The shirt

The shirt is the most basic garment. The oldest preserved shirt is 5,000 years old and is from ancient Egypt. Confusingly, it is known as the "Tarkhan Dress." Made of a striped linen, it has knife-pleated sleeves and a slim cut. The shirt is thought to have been worn by a woman or a teenager.

The Tarkhan Dress, ancient Egypt, c. 3482–3102 BCE

Shirts are made to cover the upper body, and their key features are openings for the head and arms. There are many variations of shirt. Which would you choose: Long sleeves or short? Cotton or polyester? Any pockets, ruffles, or other decorations? Would you prefer buttons or snaps? If you wear T-shirts, do you like V-necks or crew necks? There are so many options!

2. Dressing up

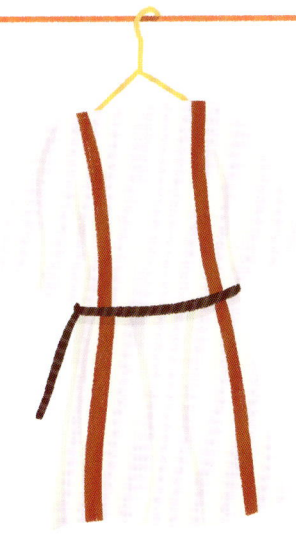

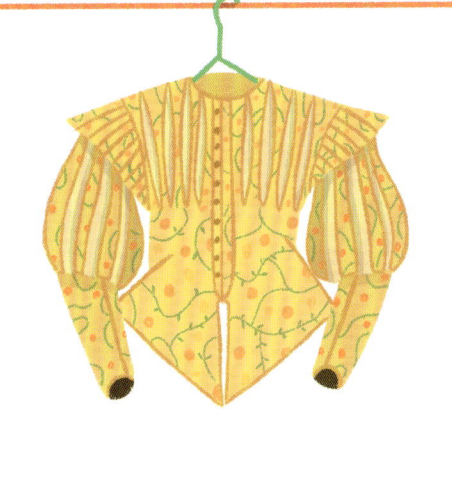

Roman tunic, c. 300 BCE

Doublet, 16th century

Frilled shirt, 17th century

Women's shirtwaister, late 19th century

Classic dress shirt, 1950s

Printed T-shirt, 1970s

For much of history, shirts were worn as nightwear or underwear, including the T-shirt. In our own time, however, T-shirts printed with slogans, pictures, or brand logos have become an important way to tell the world who we are and what we like.

The French tennis player *René Lacoste* (1904–1996) was famous in the 1920s for wearing short sleeve shirts. He used his fame to sell the first sports shirts with a logo on the front. The logo was a crocodile, which was Lacoste's nickname. If you could choose a logo, what would yours be?

2. Dressing up

Tudor dress (portrait of Queen Elizabeth I), c. 1567

Victorian dress (photograph of Omoba Aina [Sarah Forbes Bonetta]), 1862

Edwardian S-bend dress (photograph of actress Camille Clifford), c. 1900

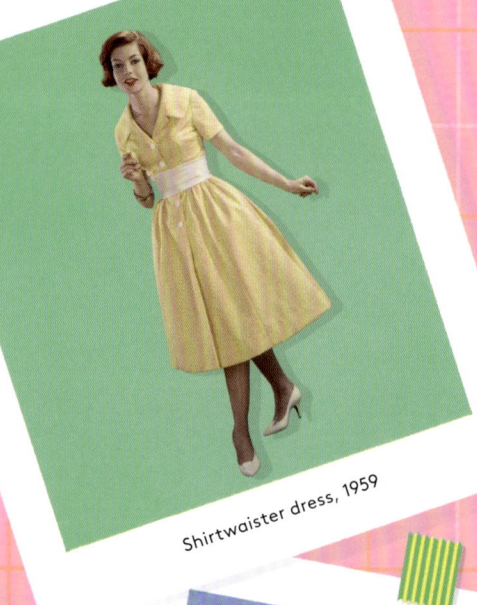

Shirtwaister dress, 1959

Embroidered caftan dress by Oscar de la Renta, 1963

Bodycon dress by Azzedine Alaïa, 2003

The dress

People of all genders have worn dresses since the beginning of recorded time. The dress is a one-piece outer garment that covers the upper body, with a skirt section over the legs. From the late Middle Ages onward, developments in how clothes were made led to European men increasingly wearing stockings, breeches, and pantaloons as outerwear, and the dress became a predominantly female garment.

The dress is probably the most creative single item in fashion history. Until the late 20th century, Western society expected women to wear dresses. Perhaps as a result, dress styles have changed more rapidly than any other garment.

Waistlines have gone in and out and in again, hemlines up and down, sleeves short or long, bodices fitted or loose, and necklines high then low. Some of these changes happen alongside developments in society and shifts in the way people think, while others are the result of new construction techniques. For example, the mass production of lighter, metal crinolines—stiff petticoats—in the mid-19th century increased the popularity of dresses with very wide, domed skirts.

In the 17th and 18th century, the fashion among the aristocracy was for really wide hips! Panniers were added under dresses to make them stick out on either side. Can you imagine trying to fit through your front door in a dress like this?

2. Dressing up

2. Dressing up

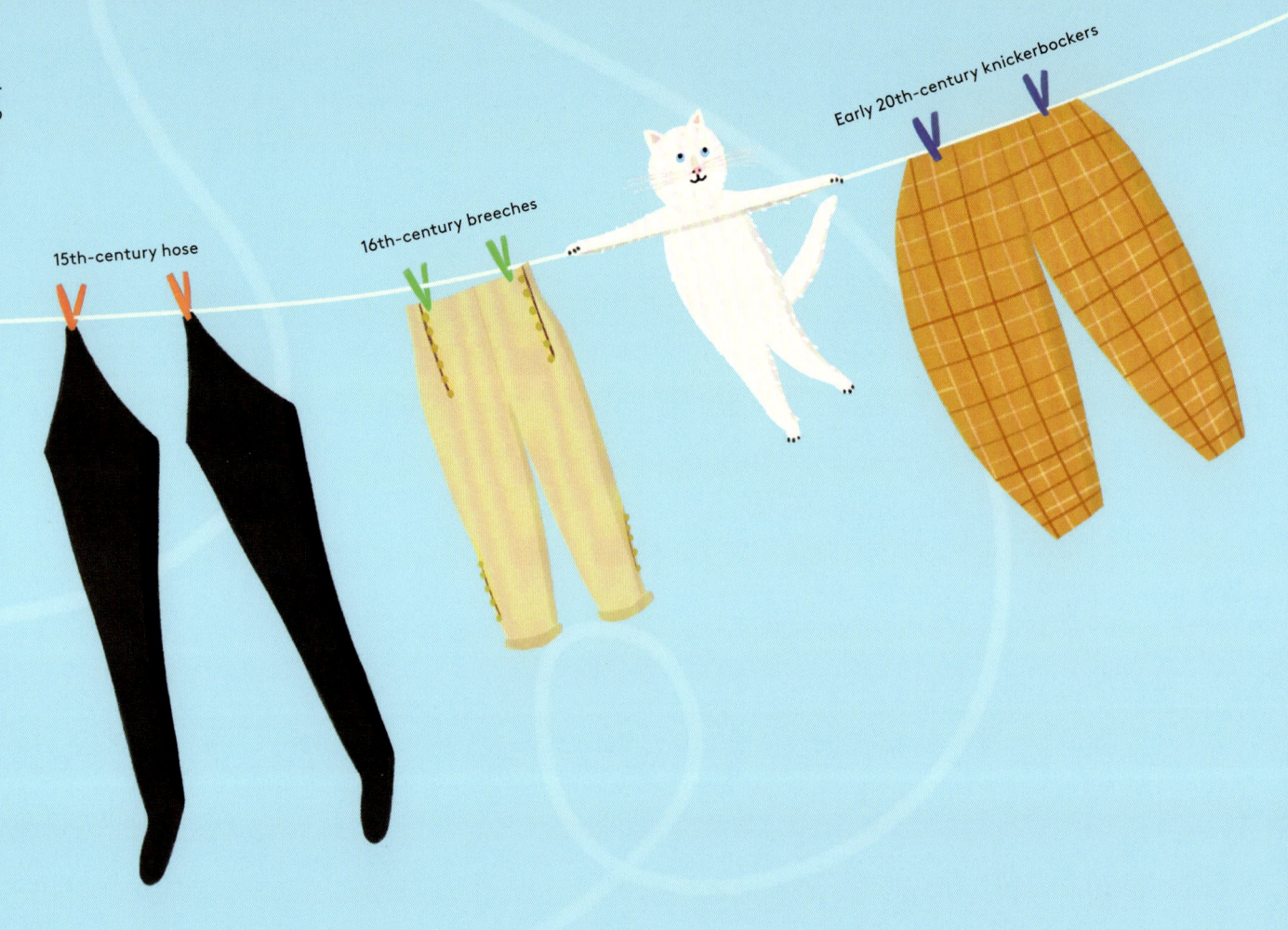

15th-century hose

16th-century breeches

Early 20th-century knickerbockers

Pants

Pants allow people to cover each leg from the waist to below the knee, and to move freely. Historians have suggested that pants developed because they made it easier for men to ride on horseback. Most societies around the world have a form of legging with fabric passing between and around the legs. But in Western countries, pants as outerwear only became standard 200 years ago.

Sometimes called breeches or britches, pantaloons, or trousers, pants were strictly menswear until the 20th century. Women began to wear bloomers underneath their dresses in the mid-1850s, but then started wearing pants for sports or workwear. The beach pajama became fashionable in the 1920s and, since then, stylish women have helped to make pants popular as casual, formal, and office wear.

1940s Savile Row suit trousers

1950s denim jeans

1970s bell-bottoms

2. Dressing up

Women dressed for the beach, 1934

25

Coats and cloaks

Coats are usually the top layer of an outfit. Although fashions change over time, there are many classic coat designs that have stayed popular and relatively unchanged for over 100 years. For example, the Chesterfield coat—a full-length overcoat with a velvet collar and either one row of buttons (single-breasted) or two rows of buttons (double-breasted)—was invented in the late 19th century, but the style is still worn today.

ELIZABETH TYLER, *Little Red Riding Hood*, c. 1919

The cloak—or its shorter version, the cape—is a sleeveless overcoat that hangs loosely from the shoulders to offer protection and warmth. Worn by ancient civilizations, referenced in religious texts, and a popular choice for both fairy tale characters and superheroes, the cape is relatively simple, and so it has never gone out of fashion.

2. Dressing up

Pelisse coat,
early 19th century

Military greatcoat,
early 20th century

Long puffer coat, 1990s

Duffle coat, 1950s

Burberry trench coat,
early 20th century

The traditional duffle coat—as worn by Paddington Bear—has toggle and rope fastenings, patch pockets, and a hood. It's named after the Belgian town of Duffel, where its thick woollen cloth was originally made. The coat was used by the army and navy and it became popular after World War II (1939–1945), when students and young people bought army surplus stock.

27

Headwear

Hats have evolved throughout the centuries not only to protect the head but also to express identity, status, and style. A traditional hat has a crown—the part that covers your head—and a brim or visor. But headwear can also be entirely unstructured, such as a headscarf.

Portrait of Emperor Shenzong of Song (1048–1085), Northern Song Dynasty, wearing a futou

An example from ancient times is the Chinese futou, a striking piece of headwear that evolved over a thousand years, from being a black knotted turban to including angular extensions worn by high-ranking officials.

Ancient Roman helmets not only protected soldiers in battle but were also a sign of their position in the army. Different ranks had different styles. Helmets with a horsehair crest running from front to back were worn by legionary officers.

2. Dressing up

In the 21st century, we still wear a wide range of hats, from traditional boaters to trendy beanies, but formal hats are rarely required. Below are just a few examples of fantastic and fashionable headgear that people wore in the past—and some that are still worn today. Which one is your favorite?

Sombrero

Bowler hat

Fez

Bonnet

Baseball cap

Beret

Top hat

Straw hat

29

2. Dressing up

Footwear

Shoes are the very definition of fashion. Their design has changed rapidly and constantly. At its most basic, all footwear is made up of three elements—the upper, the heel, and the sole. However, variations throughout history and across the globe have been endless.

Historically, footwear has been made of all sorts of materials. Some examples include shoes made of papyrus in ancient Egypt, leather sandals in ancient Rome, wooden clogs from the Netherlands, and silk slippers from China. Did you know the first rubber boots were invented in Scotland in the 1850s and renamed Wellingtons after a famous duke?

Chopines, Italy, 1550-1650

Poulaine, Europe, late 14th century

Embroidered slipper, Europe, late 17th century

Buttoned boot, US, early 20th century

Ancient Egyptian shoe, c. 1550 BCE

Geta shoe, traditional Japanese footwear

30

Shoe shapes have ranged from long, pointy shoes in the Middle Ages to the broad, squared toe that signified power in the Renaissance. In China, tiny feet were particularly prized and the painful practice of foot binding was introduced to stop the feet of young girls from growing.

The height of shoes has varied throughout history for practical as well as stylish reasons. The earliest high heels helped to keep the feet of soldiers on horseback in their stirrups.

Shoes weren't always made for left and right feet. Up until the 19th century, they were generally made "straight." Since both sides were identical, you could choose which shoe to wear on which foot!

Woman's shoes, China, Qing dynasty (1644-1911)

Dr. Martens boot, invented 1945

Nike Air Force 1 sneaker, invented 1982

Stiletto, invented 1950s

Crocs, invented 2002

2. Dressing up

THE FASHION REVOLUTION
Fashion from 1650 to 1900

I'm Louis XIV, King of France. I am very stylish and love to wear lavish and luxurious clothing. Just look at my gorgeous red-heeled shoes!

I'm Winston Churchill, a British prime minister. I buy my suits from tailors on Savile Row although I've been known to wear a boiler suit too.

I'm Jeanne Paquin, the first woman to open a Paris couture house in 1891. I'm famous for my modern designs, often inspired by different cultures and periods. I even made the color black fashionable.

3. The fashion revolution

Fashion in the city

While the importance of clothing styles existed all over the world, the industry of fashion originated in Europe and North America. During the 17th and 18th centuries, Paris started to become the world's most fashionable city. **Louis XIV** (1638–1715), who was crowned the king of France in 1643, adored luxury and opulence. Under his royal patronage, one-third of workers in Paris ended up employed in the clothing and textile trades. He even issued a declaration making it illegal for members of his court to be "unfashionable!" Personally, the king liked to wear high, red-heeled shoes.

During his reign, and in the years that followed, the clothing really didn't change much. By the 1750s, men with wealth and nobility were wearing early versions of the suit, with buttoned coats and tunics, breeches and stockings, plus powdered wigs. Women of status wore full-skirted dresses, such as the mantua and the sack-back gown (see page 37).

Next came the start of the fashion industry as we know it. Until this point, clothes were handmade by tailors and dressmakers, or by the wearers themselves. After the 1750s, fashion started to become big business in Europe and North America. This booming industry involved many elements, which included sourcing fabrics, manufacturing garments, advertising the latest fashions, and selling the goods in stores.

Woman using a spinning jenny, c. 1800

What happened to make this change? Well, innovative people came up with amazing inventions. New machinery such as the spinning jenny and the steam engine enabled textiles and clothing to be produced more quickly, efficiently, and cheaply. Factories sprang up during the "Industrial Revolution," as this period was called, and people flocked to the big cities in search of work. As business boomed, many people grew richer and could now afford to buy the new, modern goods.

Revolutionary fashion

The Industrial Revolution in the 18th century transformed the way people made and wore clothing. Britain, in particular, developed a successful textile industry. Textile mills produced cotton on a large scale, as mechanized looms were developed. This popular fabric was affordable, washable, colorfast, and could be easily printed and dyed. It could also be easily adapted to the fashions of the time.

While the Industrial Revolution led to a fashion revolution, a series of real-life revolutions were taking place in Europe and North America in the late 18th century. Monarchs were being rejected in favor of elected representatives. Sometimes, throughout history, such changes in society are accompanied by shifts in fashion.

JEAN-BAPTISTE ANDRÉ GAUTIER-DAGOTY,
Portrait of Marie-Antoinette of Austria, 1775

Marie Antoinette (1755–1793) was married to **King Louis XVI** (1754–1793) of France. Her dressmaker, **Rose Bertin** (1747–1813), is often credited as the first fashion designer, but this isn't totally accurate. Bertin didn't present finished designs to the queen; rather, they collaborated to design the elaborate outfits that Marie was known for. The queen was blamed for much of the extravagance that led to the downfall of the French monarchy.

LET THEM EAT CAKE!

Before the French Revolution in 1789, court dress was often extravagant and impractical. The most fashionable gown for women was the robe à la française (also known as a sack-back gown). This involved multiple layers, including an underskirt with padding to enlarge the hips; a decorative stomacher and petticoat; and the main dress, which was open at the front, with a voluminous panel of pleated fabric at the back. No wonder ladies of the court had servants to help them dress!

After **King Louis XVI** of France was beheaded in 1793, ostentatious Rococo fashions were replaced by the simple Empire style, inspired by the ancient Greeks and Romans. Gone were the uncomfortable wide skirts; now women wore long straight gowns of muslin (thin cotton), which fell gracefully from under the bust. Can you see how these gowns made their wearers resemble Classical statues?

Fashion designers

In the mid-1800s, the job of the fashion designer began to develop. Before this, tailors and dressmakers were commissioned to make clothing, often in collaboration with their clients. Now, fashion designers would plan and create clothing themselves, ready to present to customers.

The invention of the fashion designer is really down to one man: **Charles Frederick Worth** (1825–1895). Worth was born in England but moved to Paris in 1845. He got a job in a store selling textiles, clothing, and shawls, and he started to create dresses to display underneath the shawls. This led to him opening his own fashion salon, the *House of Worth*, in 1858. Many of Worth's innovative ideas are still with us today. For example, he presented new collections seasonally; he was the first to show his designs to his customers on live models; and he led the way in putting fashion house labels inside his clothes. Among his many celebrity clients, the stylish **Empress Eugénie** (1826–1920) of France was the most famous.

Masquerade ball dresses designed for Charles Frederick Worth, Paris, c. 1860s

3. The fashion revolution

38

By the end of the 19th century, fashion was shaped by female designers, who presented strong new ideas for women's clothing. The *Callot Sœurs* (active 1895–1937) were four sisters who found fame by working with unusual materials such as lamé and Chinese silks, as well as striking details including huge East Asian-inspired floral motifs and kimono sleeves. *Jeanne Paquin* (1869–1936) was a highly successful pioneer, who came up with innovations that included sending models dressed in her designs to public events, such as operas and horse races, to attract publicity. *Madame Chéruit* (1866–1955) was one of the first women to own and run a major French fashion house. She famously helped to launch the career of future fashion star *Paul Poiret* (see page 49). But by the second half of the 20th century, far more men than women would make their name running fashion houses.

La Côte d'Azur (A Party on the Terrace), from Gazette du Bon Ton, Summer 1915, featuring designs by Jeanne Paquin, Charles Frederick Worth, and the Callot Sœurs

Women try on dresses at The House of Worth, Paris, c. 1890s

Made to measure

In the second half of the 19th century, a new form of fashion business was created. Haute couture literally means "high sewing," and it refers to the highest level of dressmaking. Paris-based fashion couturiers of the time decided to make one-off garments that were sewn by hand to the specific measurements of a (very rich) client. The result was flawlessly crafted garments that were unique.

In order to protect this exclusive, luxury form of fashion, in 1868 *Charles Frederick Worth* (see page 38) founded what would eventually become known as the *Chambre Syndicale de la Haute Couture*. Through this institution, designers would only be able to call themselves an "haute couture house" if they met certain standards. For example, they had to have a studio in Paris that employed at least fifteen full-time members of staff. To this day, the *Chambre Syndicale* protects the status of haute couture, and exquisite garments continue to be made by hand in Paris by the most highly skilled dressmakers and tailors in the world.

While the term "haute couture" can only be used for garments that are made under *Chambre Syndicale* rules, there is another term for unique clothes that are made to measure. "Bespoke" tailoring refers to clothing that is made from scratch, according to the customer's wishes. The customer gets to choose the fabric, style, buttons, pockets, and everything else about the garment, which is then handmade by the finest tailors. This is similar to how clothes were made in the past, but the term "bespoke" has come to signify top-quality craftsmanship. It's usually associated with men's tailoring.

Stylish men would flock to centers of excellence to have their clothing made to order. No center is more famous than London's Savile Row. This little street has been home to tailors for centuries, and has hosted many notable visitors. One of its oldest establishments, *Henry Poole* & Co. (on Savile Row since 1846), has boasted clients ranging from kings and emperors to the former British prime minister **Winston Churchill** (1874–1965), who once refused to pay the tailor a rather large bill! You can still go to Savile Row today and get an item made just for you.

3. The fashion revolution

Off the peg

The invention of mechanized sewing machines in the 19th century changed the fashion industry dramatically. The sewing machine, introduced in the US in 1851 by *Isaac Singer* (1811–1875) allowed clothing to be manufactured at a much faster rate. This development enabled people to begin to purchase "off the peg" fashions (also called "ready-to-wear") directly from stores. Fashionable clothing was now available to many buyers, and most people still buy ready-made clothes from stores today.

The way people shopped changed in the 1800s. Gallerias were built to provide a pleasant shopping experience, no matter what the weather was. Many of these covered shopping streets still exist in older towns and city centers today.

By the end of the century, the department store had arrived. This was an entirely new concept in shopping. Instead of going to the dressmaker, hatmaker, shoemaker, and so on, customers could find everything they needed for a stylish outfit (and a stylish home) under one roof. Now they could see, and often touch, all the goods available. These large stores also required a lot of salespeople, and this provided new jobs for many people.

3. The fashion revolution

3. The fashion revolution

Hustle and "bustle"

Thanks to the invention of photography, excellent records exist of the clothing that people wore during the 19th century. For example, cartes de visite, which were photo postcards that could be given to friends or visitors, became hugely popular in the 1860s. So now—in addition to paintings, drawings, writing, and surviving clothing—we can look at photographs to see how people dressed.

An example of a carte de visite, c. 1887-1900

During the Victorian era (1837–1901), men's fashion largely developed into what we think of today as men's suits. The luxurious, colorful clothing worn by men in earlier eras was replaced by a more serious look. Dark jackets, pants and coats, and minimal accessories became the expected attire for men into the 20th century.

Unlike men's clothes, Victorian women's dress continued to evolve through the 19th century. When **Queen Victoria** (1819–1901) was crowned in 1837, fashionable dresses had full skirts and big sleeves. By the 1850s, huge crinolines and hoop skirts were in style. Servants had to stand on stools and use poles to get wide dresses over the wearer's head. These impractical skirts became a source of fun for cartoonists at the time. Gradually, bell-shaped crinolines were replaced with a straight skirt that had a large bustle at the back.

4

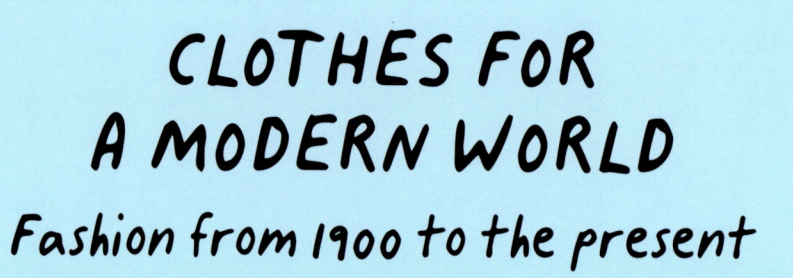

CLOTHES FOR A MODERN WORLD
Fashion from 1900 to the present

I'm Vivienne Westwood and I am wearing my iconic "GOD SAVE THE QUEEN" T-shirt. I believe fashion can ignite revolutionary ideas.

I'm Hollywood star Anna May Wong. This dragon dress is by costume designer Travis Banton.

I'm stylish movie star Audrey Hepburn. I love to wear clothes by the designer Givenchy in my movies and at award shows.

War and peace

At the turn of the 20th century, Paris was at the heart of the growing fashion industry. Stylish women traveled from across the globe, sometimes twice a year, to see the latest designs and have clothes made in the city. In 1900, a fashionable woman's wardrobe included a different outfit for every activity: a walking dress, a car coat (if traveling), an afternoon dress, a tea dress, an evening dress, and a special gown for every new occasion.

Underwear was crucial to achieving the correct look, as was a maid or servant to help tie you into it. This included a corset, which pushed breasts forward and hips back to create a fashionable S-shape in the body. But this soon became impractical for daily life.

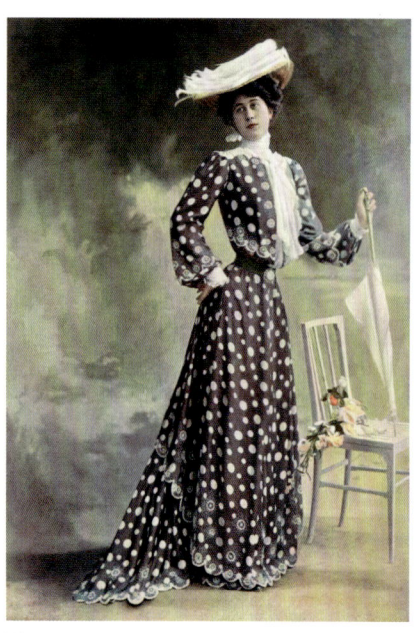

Woman wearing an S-bend promenade gown by Madeleine Laferrière, Paris, 1902

During World War I (1914–18), many women worked on farms and in factories to take the place of men who were away fighting. Clothing was at risk of getting caught in machinery, so they often wore uniforms. This practicality and comfort became important for everyday dress.

PAUL IRIBE, *Le Robes de Paul Poiret (The Dresses of Paul Poiret)*, Paris, 1908

One designer, **Paul Poiret** (1879–1944), shifted away from this stiff silhouette and promoted a softer, Eastern-inspired look. Poiret encouraged women to wear loose tunic dresses, harem pants, and hobble skirts through the drawings he commissioned and with a touring fashion show, lecture, and film.

Sport and leisure, including the new hobby of motoring, not only required women to have looser clothing but also created opportunities for men to dress colorfully and more casually. Think of the children's book character Mr. Toad in *The Wind in the Willows* (1908) sporting a straw boater and striped blazer on the river and driving an automobile in brightly checked tweeds, a flat cap, and a fur-collared coat.

4. Clothes for a modern world

The "Roaring Twenties"

After the trials of World War I (1914–18), many people embraced a new type of lifestyle, full of fun and freedom. Women designers, like the French dressmaker *Gabrielle "Coco" Chanel* (1883–1971), created clothes that allowed people to enjoy new and exciting freedoms, including jazz music, dancing, and the popular new sports of tennis, golf, and swimming. The fashionable 1920s look was a straight up-and-down silhouette. Busts were flattened and waists were hidden by loose-fitting garments. Hemlines on dresses rose to make a feature of legs and ankles, and women began to wear pants too.

Menswear also became more relaxed—especially the suit. The 1920s introduced double-breasted jackets, wide lapels, and looser pants. Good grooming included polished Oxford brogue shoes and accessories, such as a handkerchief carefully folded and displayed in a jacket pocket.

Josephine Baker dancing the Charleston at the Folies Bergère, Paris, c. 1926

Paris, where Coco Chanel had her studio, was also home to other notable fashion designers, including **Jean Patou** (1887–1936) and **Jeanne Lanvin** (1867–1946). They designed clothes in lightweight materials like chiffon, silk, and satin, with heavy decorative beads and fringing that created a sense of movement—perfect for dancing!

Style icons of the 1920s included dancers, such as **Josephine Baker** (1906–1975) and **Fred Astaire** (1899–1987). Baker's famous fringe-style dresses accentuated her fast footwork and Astaire's loose trouser legs emphasized his fluid dancing style. Their photos were reproduced widely in newspapers, magazines, and newsreels, and people copied their style.

4. Clothes for a modern world

Hollywood glamour

The 1930s began with a global financial depression and ended with the start of World War II. While many lived in extreme poverty, the key mood in fashion was grown-up glamour.

The relaxed shapes of the 1920s were replaced with structure. A typical thirties look—called the "coat hanger" silhouette—had wide, angular shoulders and a fitted waist. Skirts, which had begun to get longer by the late 1920s, now descended to the knee and mid-calf for women's everyday dress, and to the ankle for afternoon and evening wear. Shoulders were stylized with padding, sleeve caps, and halterneck details. Designers, especially **Madeleine Vionnet** (1876– 1975), cut fabric on the bias—across the grain of the fabric's weave—so that dresses curved over the body and hung in elegant folds.

Dress designed by Madeleine Vionnet, Paris, 1935

52

With the building of movie theaters in every town and city, it was possible for many people to watch a new movie every week. Hollywood storylines featured characters enjoying wealthy lifestyles and their actors promoted what to wear. Hollywood stars who wore glamorous costumes, such as *Greta Garbo* (1905–1990), *Marlene Dietrich* (1901–1992), and *Anna May Wong* (1905–1961), became style icons.

It was also a time of great technological progress. Film photography allowed fashion magazines to expand, and clothes were transformed by inventions we now take for granted like zips, synthetic fabrics, and elastic. These innovations were also used to create new types of underwear so that women could emphasize the curves they had tried to flatten in the previous decade.

4. Clothes for a modern world

4. Clothes for a modern world

Make do and mend

What to wear during a war? Fashion in the forties was dominated by the impact of World War II. From 1939 to 1945, fabric was in short supply due to wartime rationing and the need for military uniforms. In 1941, the UK government commissioned a small group of designers to create "Utility Clothing": a limited range of coats, suits, dresses, and blouses that could be manufactured efficiently with minimal cloth. People were also encouraged to "make do and mend" by fixing existing clothes.

As a result, the early 1940s silhouette was neat and modest. Women's suits included military-inspired padded shoulders, a narrow waist, and a knee-length skirt that was only slightly flared to limit the amount of fabric required. Headscarves and turbans became popular as a colorful way for women to keep their hair neat and to create a distinctive look.

4. Clothes for a modern world

With mainland Europe isolated by the Nazi Occupation, the US took the fashion lead. Taking inspiration from ballet wraps and comfortable sportswear, *Claire McCardell* (1905–1958) designed a popular wraparound dress. By wrapping the fabric around her mannequin, McCardell created the impression of a structured silhouette without the need for corsets or petticoats.

Claire McCardell designing a dress by draping fabric on a dressmaker's dummy, New York, 1940

55

The "New Look"

Time for a fresh start! In 1947, one famous fashion collection marked the end of rationing and defined postwar style. It was created by Paris couturier **Christian Dior** (1905–1957) and came to be known as the "New Look." This widely copied revolution in fashion featured elegant jackets with narrow shoulders, a defined bust, and a tightly cinched waist, as well as multilayered skirts that used luxurious amounts of fabric.

WILLY MAYWALD, The Bar suit, designed by Christian Dior, Paris, 1955

Fashion in the 1950s came to be defined by this sophistication and elegance. Paris once again became the fashion capital of the world. Refined designs by **Pierre Balmain** (1914–1982) and **Jacques Fath** (1912–1954), among others, heralded the golden age of haute couture. Successful designs were copied everywhere and could be seen in magazines, on movie screens, and on the streets.

Movie stars like **Audrey Hepburn** (1929–1993), who was often dressed by **Hubert de Givenchy** (1927–2018), wore highly feminine outfits with a cinched waist and exaggerated bust and hips. Fifties fashion, courtesy of corseted underwear and padded bras, was tailored to create and accentuate an hourglass silhouette.

In London, **Norman Hartnell** (1901–1979) and **Hardy Amies** (1909–2003) had a huge influence on women's fashion through their creations for the young **Queen Elizabeth II** (1926–2022). Meanwhile, in 1954, young designers **Karl Lagerfeld** (1933–2019) and **Yves Saint Laurent** (1936–2008) both won prizes in a Paris fashion competition. Their respective careers in haute couture and ready-to-wear changed French fashion for a generation.

New fabrics, prints, and mass manufacturing all helped the fashion industry to recover and grow after the war. In menswear, ready-to-wear suits and sports jackets imitated the elegant bespoke tailoring worn by style icons like entertainer **Sammy Davis Jr.** (1925–1990). Trends included straight-cut, slimmer pants without cuffs, single-breasted jackets with narrower lapels, and—in summer—open-necked shirts.

4. Clothes for a modern world

The space age

Welcome to the sixties: a decade of innovation and protest, marked by space exploration, supersonic flights, the Civil Rights Movement, and the Vietnam War. In fashion, a new generation of designers made bold, youthful clothes for the growing number of teenagers with money to spend.

The mini skirt and mini dress were key looks for British designer *Mary Quant* (1930–2023) and French designer *André Courrèges* (1923–2016). Typical features included an A-line shape, with zip and pocket details, and the creative use of new materials such as plastic, paper, and metal. Other key looks included the babydoll dress. This short, girlish style suited teenagers who did not want to dress like their mothers.

Yellow dress designed by André Courrèges, 1969

4. Clothes for a modern world

Hot pants were an alternative to the mini skirt and were often made in denim or suede. To complement the look, futuristic designer *Pierre Cardin* (1922–2020) introduced brightly colored tights. Models such as *Jean Shrimpton* (b. 1942) and *Twiggy* (b. 1949) became famous by promoting a childlike look that suited the fashions of the period. Young customers flocked to boutiques such as Biba, which was a new type of store selling fashionable ready-to-wear clothes. The decade had begun with exciting optimism.

Peace, love, and protest

By the late 1960s, ongoing social injustices had created a counterculture or "hippie" movement of people calling for peace and love instead of war and hate. Protesters broke the mold by wearing bell-bottom pants and tie-dyed clothing. Others rejected consumerism by wearing army surplus and secondhand clothing. Some took inspiration from Indigenous and world cultures to develop their own new individual styles. The peasant dress became popular, with its romantic wide sleeves and long skirt made from fine printed fabrics.

Many fashion designers of the 1970s drew inspiration from the past, creating their own romantic interpretations of Victorian and Edwardian styles. This nostalgic mood was fueled by books, movies, and television series. Designer **Laura Ashley** (1925–1985) became famous for her nostalgic floor-length dresses, feminine frills, floral prints, puffy sleeves, and slightly see-through fabrics.

HARRY BENSON, *Halston Four Models*, 1978

In contrast, designers like **Halston** (1932–1990) were inspired by popular disco music to encourage people to dress up and show off their bodies. Dancers at Studio 54, New York's most fashionable nightclub, typically wore close-fitting clothes that could move with the music. Flamboyant fabrics included Lurex, lamé, Lycra, silk, velvet, and fur, plus feathers and sparkling sequins. Seventies footwear featured platform soles in metallic leathers and bold colors. Popular styles included clogs, strappy sandals, and even roller skates.

In the UK, punk emerged in the 1970s. This antiestablishment music and style aimed to shock. Bands like the Sex Pistols customized everyday clothes, ripping them and scrawling slogans on them. Fashion innovator **Vivienne Westwood** (1941–2022) sold ready-made punk-style garments in her London store, including sweaters knitted so loosely they revealed the wearer's body underneath.

4. Clothes for a modern world

61

4. Clothes for a modern world

Power dressing

The eighties were all about big shoulders, big hair, and big business! The growth of corporate business across the world influenced fashion, with "power suits" becoming a key trend. These body-conscious looks had volume and emphasized an athletic body type. Catwalk shows became a talking point in popular culture in the 1980s, and it was at this time that a group of young women came to be known as the "supermodels," not only because of their fame and riches but also because they had a strong "super" silhouette. Even their hair had high volume.

Designers who responded to the showy and excessive mood of the new corporate culture included *Thierry Mugler* (1948–2022), with his spectacular broad-shouldered outfits, and *Gianni Versace* (1946–1997), who was famous for his va-va-voom glamour.

62

Pop idol **Madonna** (b. 1958) hit the headlines at the turn of the decade when she wore a pointy, cone-shaped bra-corset designed by *Jean Paul Gaultier* (see page 11). The idea of wearing underwear as outerwear was radical. Imagine wearing your underwear over your pants!

Japanese designer *Rei Kawakubo* (b. 1942) did almost the opposite: she chose to hide the shape of the body with big and baggy clothes. She was one of a group of Japanese innovators whose approach to garment construction shook up the fashion world. *Yohji Yamamoto* (b. 1943) became famous for his androgynous silhouettes in black, while *Issey Miyake* (1938–2022) won acclaim for his pleated fabrics and use of technology.

Design by Rei Kawakubo for the Comme des Garçons Fall Ready-To-Wear Collection, 1982

4. Clothes for a modern world

63

90s mixtape

Two key themes embodied nineties fashion: minimalism and antiglamour. Both were a response to the excesses of the 1980s. In fashion, minimalism refers to clean lines, neutral colors, and luxury fabrics. Designers like *Calvin Klein* (b. 1942) and *Helmut Lang* (b. 1956) pared back their garments to focus on essentials. Buttons were hidden, decoration was avoided, and the construction of the garment was made as invisible as possible. For designers including *Jil Sander* (b. 1943) and *Miuccia Prada* (b. 1949), high-tech materials and skilled cutting resulted in an elegant look that was simple but also futuristic.

Nineties supermodel Kate Moss models for the Calvin Klein Fall Ready-To-Wear Collection, 1997

In the US, the antiglamour look known as "grunge" reflected the style of the Seattle music scene and bands like Nirvana and Pearl Jam. Ripped jeans, Dr. Martens boots, Converse sneakers, cartoon T-shirts, see-through dresses, crochet cardigans, and flannel shirts were first put together on the catwalk by New York designers *Anna Sui* (b. 1955) and *Marc Jacobs* (b. 1963). Jacobs' 1992 collection for the brand Perry Ellis was criticized initially but it marked a turning point in the decade, highlighting a fresh appetite for "street style."

A different music genre, hip-hop, became popular in the mid-1990s. *Tommy Hilfiger* (b. 1951) received huge publicity when his brand, among others, was sported by hip-hop and R&B artists. Brand-new sneakers, pants worn low to reveal designer underwear, and baggy layered tops and jeans set the mood for casual style. Some of the musicians, such as *Pharrell* (b. 1973) and *50 Cent* (b. 1975), established clothing labels of their own, ahead of the widespread trend of "celebrity" design collaborations in the 21st century.

4. Clothes for a modern world

4. Clothes for a modern world

Fashion as art

Do you think fashion can be art? Well, at the beginning of the 21st century, the two worlds of fashion and art became more entwined. Museums began to embrace fashion in ways that made it more visible and accessible. In 2000, the Guggenheim Museum in New York exhibited the elegant designs of **Giorgio Armani** (b. 1934). In 2011, an exhibition called *Savage Beauty*—staged by the Metropolitan Museum of Art and dedicated to the powerful work of **Alexander McQueen** (1969–2010)—was seen by over 650,000 visitors.

Some other designers who contributed to fashion being recognized as a popular art form in the 2000s included **Tom Ford** (b. 1961), with his showstopping glamour for the red carpet; **Hedi Slimane** (b. 1968), who made menswear cool at Yves Saint Laurent and Christian Dior; and **Phoebe Philo** (b. 1973), whose sculptural chic pieces made sales spike at the house of Céline.

Giorgio Armani

Alexander McQueen

Tom Ford

How did fashion rise to art form status? There were many factors. Firstly, parts of the world—especially China and India—grew richer, which led to increased demand for the latest luxury goods. Secondly, internet speeds got faster, which meant that images and information could spread very quickly. The growth of new technologies led to improvements in the manufacture of clothing, which people could now buy online more easily. Dutch fashion designer *Iris van Herpen* (b. 1984) is well-known for her use of cutting-edge technology to help create otherworldly garments that look like something from the future.

Hedi Slimane

Design from Iris Van Herpen Fall/Winter Haute Couture Collection, 2018

Phoebe Philo

Digital generation

In the 2000s, a new generation came of age who brought a global perspective to fashion. Millennials—people born between the 1980s and the year 2000—were the first generation to grow up with the internet. They sought out many different styles as a way to express themselves through their clothes.

Also referred to as "digital natives," millennials didn't rely on traditional ways of accessing fashion. More and more, style inspiration and fashion were found online rather than in stores. Online marketplaces, like eBay (founded in 1995), were created so customers could sell items among themselves. The invention and development of smartphones and social media also created opportunities for designers and makers to work on a smaller scale, selling directly to customers.

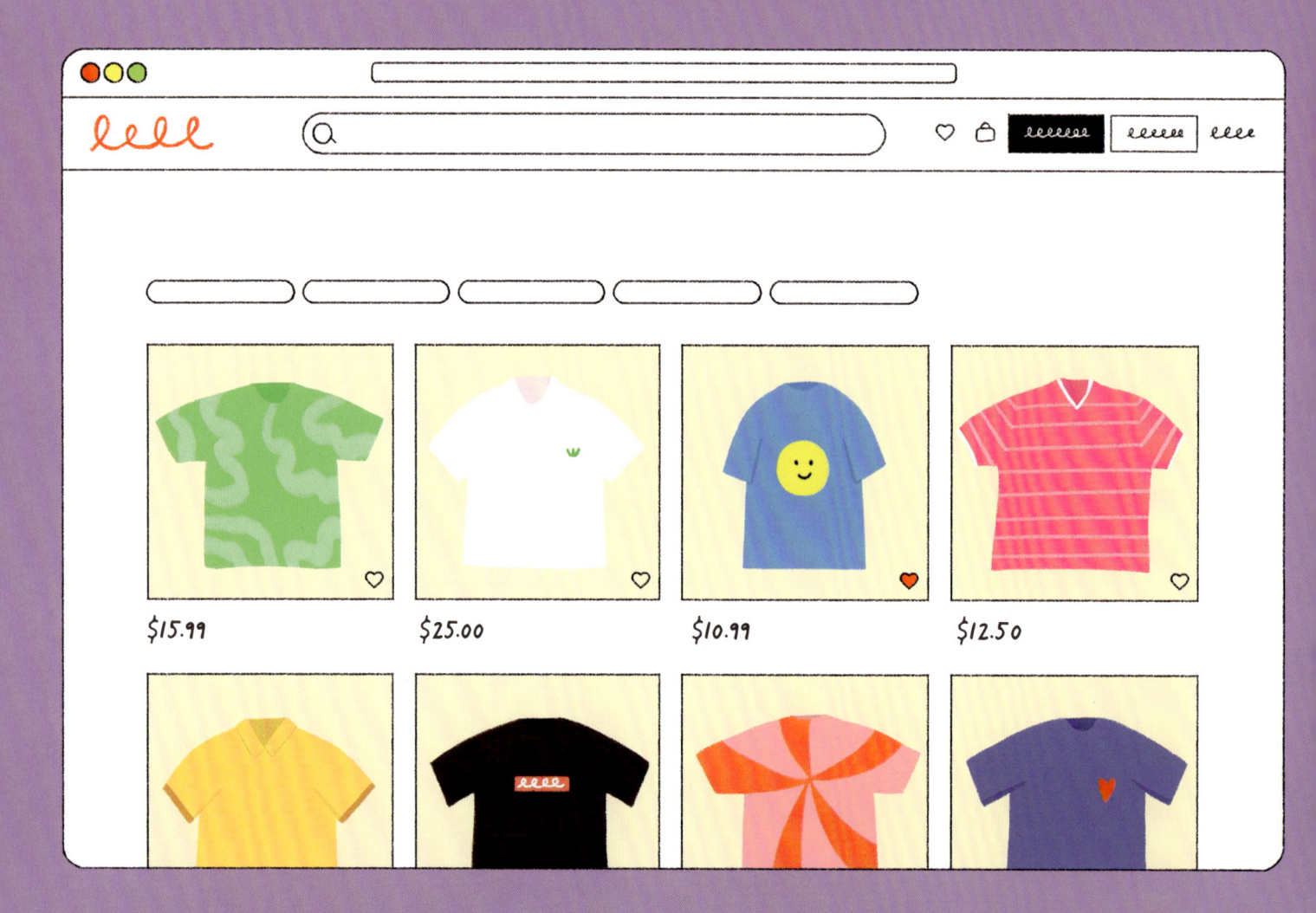

$15.99 $25.00 $10.99 $12.50

With the following generations—Gen Z and Gen Alpha—buying and selling clothing online has become even more popular. In the digital marketplace, vintage, or secondhand fashions are bought and sold as a way of changing and refreshing your closet, as well as a more environmentally friendly alternative to purchasing brand-new clothes from "fast fashion" brands.

Digital platforms and apps such as Depop and Vinted were launched to promote sales of secondhand clothing in the 2010s. These apps became particularly popular during the COVID-19 pandemic, as people at home looked to sell clothing online.

# 5

THE FASHION INDUSTRY
Makers, materials, models, and more...

I'm artist and fashion designer Jenny Kee. I love textiles with bold prints and bright colors. Can you tell from my outfit?

I'm Iris Apfel. I became a fashion icon in my old age. A Barbie doll was even made in my image. I like to have fun with how I dress and am known for my oversized glasses and flamboyant looks.

I'm famous basketball player, Michael Jordan. I'm probably as famous for my Air Jordan sneakers as I am for my slam dunks!

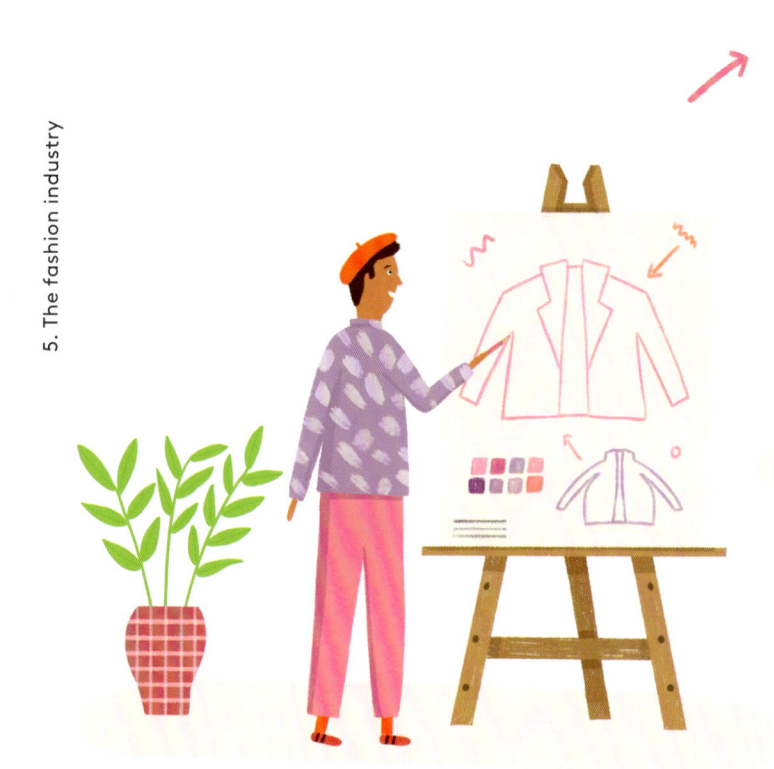

The makers

Can you make your own clothes? The stages involve choosing a design, creating a pattern, laying out your fabric, marking and cutting out the pieces, pining and sewing them together, adding any fastenings or embellishments, ironing, and finishing.

Many people in history have sewn their own clothes by hand with a needle and thread. Until the invention of the mechanical sewing machine in the 19th century (see page 42), only wealthy people could afford to have clothes made for them. Traditional roles in making clothing include weavers, pieceworkers, pattern cutters, garment and textile workers, dressmakers, and tailors. These became very specialized and highly skilled jobs over time.

The growth of mass-produced fashions involved creating large scale machinery and building garment factories—which were often unpleasant places with harsh working conditions. In fact, many modern labor laws have been written to improve the working conditions of these businesses, which are often referred to as "sweatshops." While some jobs in fashion are fulfilling and glamorous, many of the jobs sourcing fibers, making fabric, and producing the garments are not well paid.

Today, expensive, one of a kind garments are still being made by highly skilled artisans, but the vast majority of fashion is ready-to-wear clothing produced in large factories. The huge quantities of these garments—often called "fast fashion"— and their negative effect on the environment is one of the big challenges facing the fashion industry today.

Increasingly, many people are discovering the satisfaction and art of making their own clothing at home. The sale of home sewing machines has risen dramatically in recent years, and knitting and crochet are also increasing in popularity.

The fabric of fashion

Today all clothing has a label describing the fibers it is made of. Feel the clothing you are wearing and see if you can guess? Fabric can be made of natural materials, like cotton, silk, or wool; or synthetic fibers, like viscose and nylon. Sometimes they are a blend of more than one fiber, such as 50% acrylic and 50% wool.

The earliest fabrics were made from linen. Museums have examples from civilizations dating back thousands of years (see page 20). To create linen, fibers from the flax plant are harvested and spun into yarn. Strands of yarn are then woven together on a loom to create fabric.

Wool is sourced from sheep. Their fleeces are sheared and put through a process of combing, cleaning, and carding before it can be spun into yarn and dyed different colors. Woollen yarn can then be woven into fabric, or knitted or crocheted into garments.

Other animal fibers used in textiles include angora—which comes from the fur of a special rabbit—and mohair, which is from a goat. While some animals, like sheep, benefit from being sheered, other animals are sometimes harmed or killed in the process of collecting their fur. Some people avoid wearing fabric that comes from animals because of this.

A woman spins Angora rabbit wool in her garden, 1930

Human ingenuity has created new methods and materials. Inventions such as **William Lee's** (1563–1614) stocking frame from 1589 and **Eli Whitney's** (1765–1825) mechanical cotton gin, invented in 1793, helped to create textiles faster. Experiments with new types of synthetic fiber have helped to make textiles cheaper. Rayon is derived from wood pulp and was created in the 19th century as a cheaper alternative to silk. Polyester is a textile made from oil, air, and water that is used widely in fashion and accessories today. While it is colorfast, shrink- and wrinkle-resistant, and dries quickly, it is damaging to the environment as it doesn't break down, and can pollute water when it is washed.

In the late 1980s, the Japanese designer **Issey Miyake** (see page 63) and his design team developed a new pleated fabric from polyester. Clothes were sewn and then pleated in a machine. These garments were lightweight, wrinkle-resistant, and fit a wide range of people. Miyake patented his pleating technique in 1993, launching the Pleats Please Collection.

Pattern and print

Printed textiles bring color, pattern, and imagery to clothes and accessories. The oldest printing method is woodblock—where a design is carved into a wooden block, coated in ink and then pressed onto fabric to transfer the design. Other processes include roller printing, screen printing, and heat transfer. In the 21st century, digital technology has allowed designers to use print in clever new ways.

Hand-painted and printed cotton textiles became popular in the 16th and 17th century when they were imported from India to Europe. In fact, they became so popular the English government banned these textiles, as they were hurting the local textile industry. Indian textile prints remained expensive but by the mid-18th century European companies were successfully block printing cheaper copies.

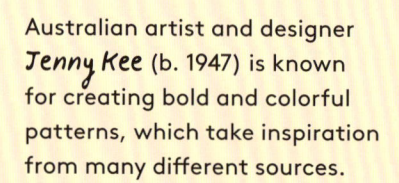

Australian artist and designer *Jenny Kee* (b. 1947) is known for creating bold and colorful patterns, which take inspiration from many different sources.

A pattern is a repeated design. In addition to floral chintzes, popular fashion fabric patterns include geometric stripes, tartans, checks, dots, paisleys, chinoiserie, and doodles. Today, people train to be textile designers to produce new and exciting fabric patterns.

Tartan fabric

Sonia Delaunay

Marimekko

5. The fashion industry

Liberty pattern

Emilio Pucci

Andy Warhol

Polka-dot fabric

Striped fabric

Althea McNish

Unlike fashion brands, textile designers for fashion are often anonymous. Yet some companies have created a name by producing and selling prints internationally, including Vlisco (founded 1846), Liberty of London (founded 1875), Bianchini-Férier (founded 1888), Marimekko (founded 1951), and Laura Ashley (founded 1953). Individual designers such as **Emilio Pucci** (1914-92), **Sudo Reiko** (b. 1953), and **Mary Katrantzou** (b. 1983) are known for pushing the boundaries of creativity and production.

Some artists, including **Sonia Delaunay** (1885-1979), **Althea McNish** (1924–2020), and **Andy Warhol** (1928-1987), have had their work applied to fashion fabrics.

5. The fashion industry

The media

Who is the best-dressed person you know? There are always people with a real eye for fashion. Throughout the decades we have looked to them for ideas on how to dress. Famous people—featured in print or on screen—have often taken the lead. Some have even founded their own fashion companies, or have collaborated with well-known brands. When the athlete **Michael Jordan** (b. 1963) was photographed wearing his colorful Air Jordan sneakers on the basketball court in the mid-1980s, his partnership with Nike made him world-famous.

The world of movies has also embraced the world of fashion. Costume designers have provided many fashion "moments" for movie stars and their characters. Notable recent examples include the outfits made for the citizens of Wakanda in *Black Panther* (2018), which were inspired by both traditional and contemporary African fashions; the dramatic gowns worn by the notorious villain in *Cruella* (2021); and the nostalgic and colorful wardrobe of the iconic doll in *Barbie* (2023). Meanwhile, the red carpets of movie premieres and award ceremonies have also become major fashion events.

Magazines have also given people ideas on how to dress. Fashion magazines began in the late 1700s—first showing drawings of outfits, known as "fashion plates," then later showing photographs of outfits styled by fashion editors and worn by models. The world's most famous fashion magazine is *Vogue*. From the 2000s onward, *Vogue* began to feature celebrities on its covers, rather than models. This move reflected a wider trend in society: actors, musicians, and personalities were now style influencers around the world.

Today, it is possible for anyone to establish a career through an individual sense of style. Technology has developed—from photography and movies to television and the internet—so that we can now create and share inspiring images instantly, whenever we want, on our phones and computers.

Where will we find the influencers of tomorrow? Will we still look to social media, magazines, movies, and newspapers? Or will we find inspiration elsewhere?

Sustainability

The fashion industry is one of the biggest businesses in the world. Over 100 billion garments are made every year. While this brings employment to millions of people, it also has an impact on our planet.

Many of our materials and processes cause problems. For example, cotton is a natural fiber but it takes a huge amount of precious water to grow the plants and produce the cotton fabrics. Similarly, some synthetic fibers last a long time, dry quickly, and don't stain easily, but they also release harmful microplastics into the environment.

In addition, we as consumers are buying more clothes than ever before. Did you know the average person only wears thirty percent of the clothes they own? We can all buy fewer clothes and think carefully about the ones we do buy. For example, we can "shop local," supporting our local communities and small businesses. Or we can borrow our clothes from rental websites, instead of owning them. We can also repair them when they need fixing. Can you think of other ways to reduce your clothing consumption?

Vivienne Westwood at London Fashion Week, London, 2013

In 2012, at the London Paralympics closing ceremony, fashion designer *Vivienne Westwood* (see page 61) announced the Climate Revolution. Her aim was to make politicians and businesspeople take action on environmental issues.

At the moment, there are two common modes of consuming fashion. The first is to buy clothes and then throw them away when they are worn out or no longer wanted. The second involves recycling: we buy clothes then give them to a recycling center or secondhand store, but they still get thrown away eventually.

Leaders in the fashion industry, however, are working on a third option. If we can adopt a "circular" system, where clothes are never thrown away, we will be able to help our planet. We won't need to wear out the soil and use up so much water, and we won't need to deal with millions of tons of waste polluting our land and oceans. Instead, we can make clothes, use and reuse them, remake them into different garments or products, recycle them into raw materials, then use those raw materials to once again make clothes, use them, and so on. By using the same materials over and over again, we can help to create sustainable fashion far into the future!

On trend

So what's new? There are two types of trend in fashion. The first relates to new looks that become fashionable for a short period of time. You might notice, say, that a particular style of jeans is suddenly everywhere. The second type of trend relates to new attitudes that society is taking. You might see, for example, more stores selling unisex fashion instead of having separate sections for boys and girls, or more clothing being made from recycled or sustainable materials. How do stores know about new trends? There are many ways. One way is to look to society and copy influencers and trendsetting people on city streets.

Stores might also be inspired by what famous designers are showing on the catwalk. In the best-known fashion cities in the world—Paris, New York, London, and Milan—new designs for Fall/Winter are traditionally presented at the start of the year and new looks for Spring/Summer at the end of the year. This means that before the real-life seasons begin there is time for stores to order the clothes, for magazines to photograph the new looks, and for manufacturers to produce the orders.

5. The fashion industry

In addition to the "official" fashion calendar, a fashion show probably takes place somewhere in the world every week of the year! Inspiring designs are now shown all over the globe, from Tokyo (Japan) and Mumbai (India) to Dakar (Senegal) and Lagos (Nigeria).

Models walk for Christian Dior's Fall Collection, Mumbai, 2023

Another way for the fashion industry to look out for new trends is to collaborate with people who work as "trend forecasters." They gather information on the industry and on people's lifestyles, then they use this data to make predictions about the styles, colors, fabrics, textures, and accessories that fashion designers might like to think about for their next collections.

83

Is fashion for everyone?

Historically, fashion has often held a narrow view of beauty. For a long time, models were almost always young, slim, able-bodied people, and most of them were white. This meant that a lot of people would never see anyone that looked like them on a catwalk or in fashion magazines and advertising.

What's more, most fashion brands, and stores would only make and stock a very limited range of sizes, which excluded many people from wearing their clothes. Does that sound fair to you?

Luckily, many brands are now working to make fashion more inclusive for people of every race, ethnicity, body type, ability, size, age, and gender identity. Fashion shows and campaigns now often feature a diverse cast of models, celebrating different forms of beauty, and brands are becoming more "size inclusive" by increasing their range of sizes.

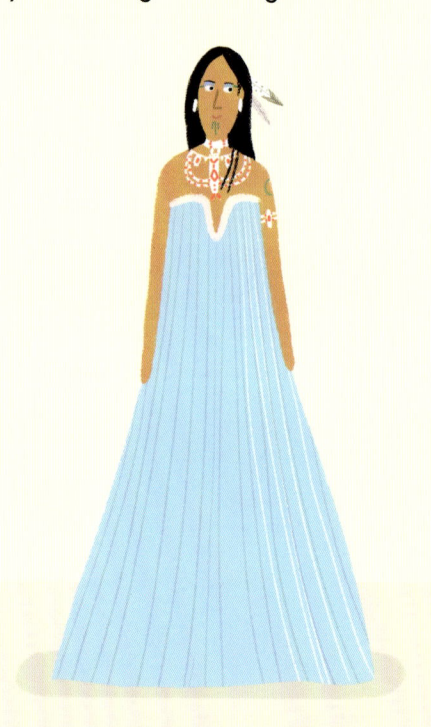

Quannah Chasinghorse (b. 2002) is a successful model. She is Native American, from the Hän Gwich'in and Oglala Lakota peoples, and proudly bears the facial tattoos of her heritage.

Iris Apfel (1921–2024) became a fashion icon when she was nearly 100 years old. She once said, "You might as well have a little fun when you dress." This sounds like excellent advice!

5. The fashion industry

In 2018, *Aaron Rose Philip* (b. 2001) became the first Black, transgender model with a physical disability to sign to a major modeling agency. In 2021, she became the first model to use a wheelchair on the catwalk for a luxury brand at the Moschino Spring/Summer 2022 Collection.

Sinéad Burke (b. 1990) is a writer, activist, and Disabled educator who champions design that includes everyone. She has advised major global fashion brands and has written articles for *Vogue*. In 2019 she became the first little person to appear on the magazine's cover.

While there is still a long way to go to make fashion truly inclusive for people with disabilities, brands including Tommy Hilfiger and Nike have introduced "adaptive fashion" to their lines—fashionable clothing designed for the diverse needs of people with disabilities.

Did you know that until the 1940s pink was considered a color for boys and blue for girls? Recently, there has been a rise in unisex and gender-fluid fashion, as brands make clothes that anybody can wear, no matter their gender.

So, is fashion now for everyone? While great changes have been made, there is still more to do. Some people still struggle to find fashionable clothes that fit. Not only should we be seeing people from all walks of life represented in advertising, but across the whole fashion industry. From designers to photographers, stylists to business owners—the more diverse fashion becomes, the more innovative, fun, and fair it will be!

5. The fashion industry

The history of fashion... to be continued

The story of fashion—of how and why we get dressed and what we wear—is a story that is continually being written. As we change along with society, so do our clothes.

Fashion history tells us about our past. It reveals where we have come from, since clothing often reflects the ideas, events, and technologies of the times when they were worn. In this way, we can look at historical garments around the world and read the many different stories they contain.

For example, the history of fashion in the early 21st century can be read in two ways. Firstly, from the top-down: famous fashion designers at expensive brands were creating distinctive looks both on the catwalk and in their advertisements. Secondly, from the bottom-up: ordinary people were mixing up affordable and secondhand clothing to create unique and inexpensive street styles.

5. The fashion industry

Right now, there's a movement to support fashion that protects the planet. When the British designer *Stella McCartney* (b. 1971) launched her brand in 2001, she set out to design fashion that would not harm the environment or animal rights. She banned the use of leather, fur, and feathers in her products. Her label was one of the first to have a sustainability policy, which means she tries to use as few of Earth's resources as possible. Many other brands are now taking similar steps to become more eco-conscious.

What is our future story of fashion? The answer is as much about individual people as it is about the global fashion industry. The story of fashion is personal—it's your story.

When you look in the closet and pick something to wear, you are writing another page in your fashion story. What will you wear today? What about tomorrow?

TIMELINE OF INVENTIONS

BCE stands for "Before the Common Era"
c. stands for "circa" and means "approximately"

Historians originally thought that Jesus was born in the year 1, at the start of the Common Era. Events that occurred before his birth are counted back from that year, and events after his birth are counted forward.

c. 8000 BCE
The ancient Egyptians are making linen from flax plants. Linen is cool and lightweight—perfect for Egypt's hot climate.

c. 3000 BCE
The Chinese are spinning silk from silkworm cocoons. The method is a closely guarded secret, known only in China.

c. 2000 BCE
The Indus Valley Civilization (modern-day Pakistan) is credited with the invention of the button. These were often made from seashells.

c. 215 BCE
Ancient Rome issues the first sumptuary law, limiting women's wearing of multicolored tunics and ownership of gold.

c. 1400s
The idea of "fashion" begins to form. For the first time in human history, one's clothing can be judged as "out of date."

1770
James Hargreaves patents his spinning jenny, which revolutionizes the production of cotton yarn.

88

1838

Le Bon Marché is founded in Paris, selling a variety of goods. It's widely credited as the first modern department store.

1846

Henry Poole opens the first tailoring business on Savile Row in London. The street remains the center of men's tailoring.

1851

Isaac Singer obtains a patent to simplify the sewing machine, leading to its mass production and use in the home.

1856

William Henry Perkin accidentally discovers a dye that produces a vivid purple. This marks the start of synthetic dyeing.

1858

Charles Frederick Worth opens his fashion house in Paris. He is widely considered to be the "father of haute couture."

1892

Fashion magazines started to appear from the late 18th century onward. *Vogue* is the most famous, first published on December 17, 1892.

TIMELINE OF INVENTIONS

1926
Gabrielle "Coco" Chanel designs a simple black dress. Her idea of the "Little Black Dress" has never gone out of fashion.

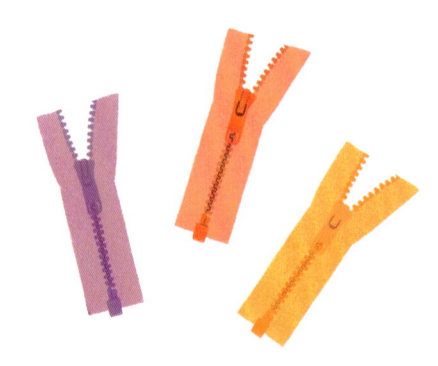

1935
Elsa Schiaparelli is the first designer to use the zip for fashion, using plastic versions in many colors.

1938
Nylon, the first successful synthetic polymer fabric, is patented. Its first use is for women's stockings.

1947
Fashion designer Christian Dior debuts his "New Look." The tiny-waisted full-skirted silhouette transforms fashion overnight.

1955
Swiss engineer George de Mestral patents Velcro, the first "touch fastener" in history. It's named after "velvet" and "crochet."

1958
Spandex (also known by its commercial name Lycra) is invented. Stretchy and strong, it radically improves sportswear.

1965

The term "mini skirt" is first used to refer to popular short skirts. Mary Quant likely coined the name after the Mini Cooper car.

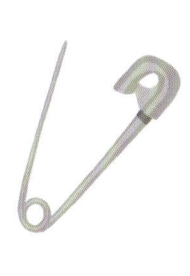

1977

Punk music inspires provocative fashion. Zandra Rhodes uses safety pins (patented 1849) in her Conceptual Chic Collection.

1983

January 1: the unofficial birthday of the internet. It has since developed so people can now see, share, and buy anything, anywhere, at any time.

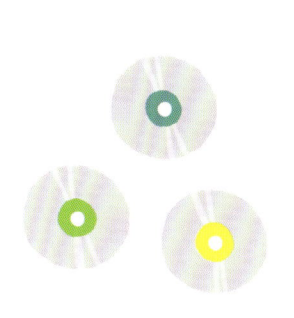

1998

Helmut Lang presents the first "virtual fashion show" for one of his collections, releasing it on the internet and CD-ROM.

2009

New sustainable leather alternatives made from mycelium, the rootlike system of mushrooms, are invented.

2010

The social media app Instagram launches and becomes one of many tools for brands and influencers to share fashion with a global audience.

GLOSSARY

ACCESSORIES items worn for decoration, such as jewelry, watches, gloves, hats, or scarves.

ANDROGYNOUS appearing both masculine and feminine.

CATWALK a platform or runway used for fashion shows.

CHIC a French word used to describe smart, elegant, and sophisticated fashion.

CHIFFON a very light fabric made from silk or nylon, often used to make light scarves or flowing skirts.

CONSPICUOUS CONSUMPTION the deliberate buying and displaying of expensive and desirable items, such as designer clothing, to show off wealth and prestige.

COLORFAST used to describe a dyed material whose color will not fade or run over time or with washing.

CORSET a tight-fitting undergarment typically worn by women between the chest and hips, to support the bust and shape the waist.

COTTON a soft, light fabric made from the seedpod fibers of the cotton plant. It is used to create other types of fabric such as denim or flannel.

DEPARTMENT STORE a large store that sells a wide range of items sorted into different areas or "departments."

DOUBLET a style of men's jacket popular from the Middle Ages to the 17th century.

DYE a plant or chemical used to add color to fabric or clothes.

GENDER-FLUID describes a gender identity that changes over time and can shift outside of or between the binary "male" or "female."

HAUTE COUTURE French for "high sewing" or "high dressmaking," referring to expensive and unique fashion pieces made by the most experienced designers.

HEMLINE the lowest edges of a garment.

HIGH FASHION brand new and expensive fashion pieces made by acclaimed designers, usually worn by celebrities and the very wealthy.

IDENTITY who a person is, made up of the traits and beliefs that are most important to them, such as gender identity, race, sexuality, or religion. Fashion is one way of visually expressing identity.

INCLUSIVE describes something that is made for, or features, many different types of people. This could include showing a wide range of races, body types, abilities, ages, genders, or sexualities.

INDIGENOUS the native people of a country or area of land.

KNICKERBOCKERS loose pants that gather below the knee.

LACE a delicate fabric made by twisting and knitting cotton or silk threads into patterns. The gaps between the fabric are as much a part of the lace design as the fabric itself.

LAMÉ a woven or knitted fabric featuring fine metallic yarns such as gold, silver, or copper with a shimmery appearance. It is often used to make evening wear and theatrical costumes.

LOGO a symbol for a company or product, such as the designer of a piece of clothing, that is shown as part of the design.

LUREX metallic-coated yarns patented in the mid-20th century that add shine to various textiles.

LUXURY something that is desirable but not necessary or essential. Luxury fashion is considered to be particularly smart or elegant, but very expensive.

LYCRA a brand of elasticized fabric invented in the 1960s that is used in stretchy figure-hugging garments and sportswear.

MANTUA a loose women's gown worn over layers of underwear in the late 17th to 18th century.

MICROPLASTICS tiny pieces of plastic created by the breakdown of products containing plastic. They are harmful to the environment.

MODEL a person who wears and displays clothes and accessories at fashion shows and in photographs.

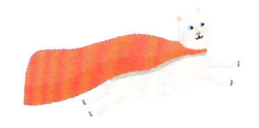

NATIONAL COSTUME a traditional or ceremonial outfit associated with a country or region, often worn for important celebrations.

NOSTALGIC describes something that deliberately reminds people of a historic period or style.

PAPYRUS a grass plant with fibrous stems. In ancient Egypt, these plant fibers were used to make paper and fabric.

PATENT a legal right granted to a person or company for an invention or design. Once something is patented, only the owner of the patent is allowed to make or sell it.

PATTERN (dressmaking) a template used to cut fabric pieces to the correct size and shape before they are assembled into clothing.

PETTICOAT an undergarment worn beneath a skirt or dress.

POLYESTER a synthetic fiber made from plastic, used to make a wide variety of garments.

SATIN a type of fabric where the warp yarns are more visible than the weft to give a smooth feel.

READY-TO-WEAR clothing made and sold in standard sizes. First introduced by couture houses as a cheaper alternative to haute couture in the 1960s.

SHIRTWAISTER a woman's blouse or dress, with details that resemble a men's shirt.

SILHOUETTE in fashion and clothing, this term refers to the overall outline or shape of a garment.

SILK a strong, lustrous fiber from the unwound cocoon of a silkworm, used to create yarn and weave fabric. Silk garments are often expensive due to the time and skills involved in making them.

SPINNING JENNY a machine used to spin large quantities of wool or cotton.

STOMACHER a V-shaped panel of decorative fabric, worn mostly by women across the front of a gown to achieve a corset-like effect. Popular from the late Middle Ages to the 18th century.

STREETWEAR a casual clothing style that became popular in the 1990s. Influenced by hip-hop, skate, and surf culture in the US, streetwear incorporates loose, comfortable items such as hoodies, sweatpants, and sneakers.

SUMPTUARY LAWS laws that restrict how much money a person can spend on expensive and luxury items.

SUSTAINABLE using as few of Earth's resources as possible.

SWEATSHOPS factories where large numbers of garments are made cheaply and quickly. The working conditions in these factories are often harsh and unpleasant and their workers are poorly paid.

SYNTHETIC a substance made chemically, by humans, to imitate a natural substance such as a plant fiber.

TAILORING the process of creating clothing or an outfit that specifically fits a customer.

TEXTILE a fabric or cloth.

TIE-DYE a coloring process that involves tying or blocking off parts of a fabric before dyeing to create a pattern.

TRANSGENDER when a person's gender identity does not match the sex they were assigned at birth.

TUNIC a simple slip-on garment that covers the torso.

TURBAN a head covering—traditionally worn by men—made of one long strip of material that is wrapped around the head.

UNIFORM matching clothing that is worn by all members of an organization, such as the army, or people attending a group or institution, such as a school.

UNISEX suitable for any gender.

VELVET a thick, soft fabric that is smooth to the touch. It is often used in evening wear; comfortable garments such as dressing gowns; or accessories such as hats, gloves, and scarves.

LIST OF ILLUSTRATIONS

a = above, b = below, c = center,
l = left, r = right

Dimensions are given in centimeters, followed by inches

page 12: Torii Kiyonaga, Kanjo: A Court Lady, c.1790. Woodblock print, 38.1 x 25.4 cm. (15 x 10 in.). The Howard Mansfield Collection, Purchase, Rogers Fund, 1936. The Metropolitan Museum of Art, New York (JP2615)

page 20: The Tarkhan Dress, ancient Egypt, c. 3482–3102 BCE, linen. Petrie Museum of Egyptian Archaeology, UCL, London (LDUCE-UC28614a-j). Photo Courtesy of The Petrie Museum of Egyptian and Sudanese Archaeology, UCL

page 22al: Steven van der Meulen, Portrait of Queen Elizabeth I, c.1567. Oil on canvas, transferred from panel, 196 x 140 cm. (77 ¼ x 55 ⅛ in.). Private Collection

page 22ar: Camille Silvy, Portrait of Sarah Davies (née Forbes Bonetta), 1862. Albumen print, 8.3 x 5.6 cm. (3 ¼ x 2 ¼ in.). National Portrait Gallery, London (NPG Ax61380)

page 22cl: Camille Clifford, Danish-born actress, c.1900. Photo Popperfoto/Getty Images

page 23cr: Fashion model wearing a yellow shirtwaister dress, London, 1959. Photo Popperfoto/Getty Images

page 22 bl: Evening caftan from Oscar de la Renta, New York, 1963. Photo Associated Press/Alamy

page 22 br: A model on the runway at the Azzedine Alaïa Spring 2003 show in Paris. Photo Giovanni Giannoni/WWD/Penske Media/Getty Images

page 25: Women dressed for the beach, 1934. Photo Hulton-Deutsch Collection/Corbis/ Getty Images

page 26: Elizabeth Tyler, Little Red Riding Hood, c.1919. Print, 59 x 44 cm. (23 ¼ x 17 ⅜ in.). National Child Welfare Association, Lawrence Public Library, Lawrence, MA (LH 2015.14)

page 28: Unknown artist, Emperor Shenzong of Song, Northern Song dynasty (960-1127 CE). Hanging scroll, ink and color on silk, 176.4 x 114.4 cm. (69 ½ x 45 ⅛ in.). Palace Museum, Taipei

page 30: Chopines, Italian, 1550–1650. Silk, metal. Brooklyn Museum Costume Collection at The Metropolitan Museum of Art, Gift of the Brooklyn Museum, 2009; Gift of Herman Delman, 1955. The Metropolitan Museum of Art, New York (2009.300.1494a, b)

page 31: Woman's shoes, China, Qing dynasty (1644–1911). Blue and red sateen, gilt trim. Bequest of Frank S. Brewer, Art Institute of Chicago (1937.391a-b)

page 35: Woman using a spinning jenny, c.1880. Colorized print. Photo The Print Collector/ Heritage Images/Alamy

page 36: Jean-Baptiste André Gautier-Dagoty, Portrait of Marie-Antoinette of Austria, 1775. Oil on canvas, 162 x 130.3 cm. (63 ⅞ x 51 ⅜ in.). Palace of Versailles Collections (MV 8061)

page 38: Masquerade ball dresses designed for Charles Frederick Worth, Paris, c.1860s. Watercolor and pencil drawing, 21.5 x 12.5 cm. (8 ½ x 5 in.). Given by the House of Worth, Victoria and Albert Museum, London (E.22072-1957 & E.22046-1957)

page 39: La Côte d'Azur (A Party on the Terrace), from Gazette du Bon Ton, Summer 1915, No. 8-9. On loan from the MA Ghering-van Ierlant Collection, Rijksmuseum, Amsterdam (RP-P-2009-3655)

page 40: Women try on dresses at Maison Worth (Worth Fashion House), Paris, c.1890s, after a watercolor by Lionello Balestrieri, published in Das XIX. Jahrhundert in Wort und Bild, Deutsches Verlagshaus Bong, Berlin, 1898

page 44: J. P. Ball & Son, Unidentified Woman, c.1887-1900, carte de visite. Gelatin silver print, 16.5 × 10.8 cm. (6 ½ × 4 ¼ in.). Collection of the Smithsonian National Museum of African American History and Culture, Washington, DC (2014.37.28.53)

page 48: Woman wearing an S-shape promenade gown by Madeleine Laferrière, Paris, 1902. Color plate from Les Modes. Photo Paul Popper/Popperfoto/Getty Images

page 49: Paul Iribe, Les Robes de Paul Poiret (The Dresses of Paul Poiret). Pochoir plate with hand-coloring, 33.8 x 31.9 cm. (13 ⅜ x 12 ⅝ in.). Published by Paul Poiret, Paris, 1908

page 51: Josephine Baker dancing the Charleston at the Folies Bergère, Paris, c.1926. Photograph Stanisław Julian Ignacy Ostroróg. Gelatin silver print, 30 × 21.1 cm. (11 13⁄16 × 8 5⁄16 in.). Gift from Jean-Claude Baker, Collection of the Smithsonian National Museum of African American History and Culture, Washington, DC (2016.135.2)

page 52: Dress designed by Madeleine Vionnet, Paris, 1935. Photo Boris Lipnitzki/Roger-Viollet/ TopFoto

page 55: Claire McCardell designs a dress by draping fabric on a dressmaker's dummy, New York, 1940. Photo Bettmann/Getty Images

page 56: Willy Maywald, Christian Dior's 1947 Bar suit, modeled by Renée Barton, Paris, 1955. Photograph © Association Willy Maywald/ADAGP, Paris and DACS, London 2025

page 58: Yellow dress designed by Andrew Courrèges, 1969. Photograph Bert Stern for *Vogue*, March 1969. Photo Bert Stern/Condé Nast/Getty Images

page 61: Harry Benson, Halston Four Models, 1978. Archival pigment print. Photo © Harry Benson

page 63: Design by Rei Kawakubo for the Comme des Garçons Fall Ready-To-Wear Collection, 1982. Model Dalma Callado. Photograph Guy Marineau for WWD magazine. Photo Guy Marineau/WWD/ Penske Media/Getty Images

page 64: Kate Moss models for the Calvin Klein Fall Ready-To-Wear Collection, 1997. Photo David Turner/Penske Media/Getty Images

page 67: Design from Iris Van Herpen Fall/Winter Haute Couture Collection, Paris, 2018. Photo Jonas Gustavsson/Sipa US/Alamy

page 75: A woman spins Angora rabbit wool in her garden, 1930. Photo Fox Photos/Getty Images

page 77al: Tartan fabric. Photo rangizzz/ Adobe Stock

page 77ac: Sonia Delaunay, Composition, 1956. Handwoven Aubusson wool tapestry, 186.1 x 149.9 cm. (73 ⅜ x 59 ⅛ in.). Private Collection. Photo Christie's Images/Bridgeman Images. © Pracusa

page 77ar: Unikko by Maija Isola, signature pattern for the brand Marimekko. Photo courtesy Marimekko

page 77cl: Tana Lawn™ cotton fabric, Liberty Fabrics' most iconic prints. Permission of Liberty Fabric Limited

page 77c: PUCCI, Onde pattern printed silk twill scarf. Courtesy NET-A-PORTER

page 77cr: Andy Warhol, Ice Cream Desserts, c.1959. Cotton textile. © 2025 The Andy Warhol Foundation for the Visual Arts, Inc./Licensed by DACS, London

page 77bl: Polka-dot fabric. Photo Dmytro Synelnychenko/Adobe Stock

page 77bc: Striped fabric. Photo naataali/ Adobe Stock

page 77br: Althea McNish, Van Gogh textile, 1959. Screen-printed cotton, 142.2 x 125.7 cm. (56 x 49 ½ in.). Committee on Architecture and Design Funds. Museum of Modern Art (MoMA), New York, US. Photo The Museum of Modern Art, New York/Scala, Florence

page 80: Vivienne Westwood showcases her Spring/Summer 2013 Collection during London Fashion Week on September 16, 2012. Photo Gareth Cattermole/Getty Images

page 83: Models walk for Christian Dior's Fall Collection, Mumbai, March 30, 2023. Photo Indranil Mukherjee/AFP/Getty Images

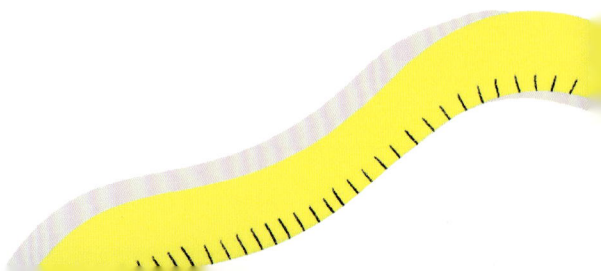

INDEX

accessories 15, 50, 92
adaptive fashion 85
androgynous 63, 92
antiglamour 64

boutique 59
breeches 23, 24, 34
buttons 14, 26, 64, 88

capes 13, 26
cartes de visite 44
catwalk 62, 84–85, 92
chic 66, 92
chiffon 51, 92
coats 26–27, 34, 44, 54
colorfast 36, 92
conspicuous consumption 13, 92
corset 48, 57, 63, 92
cotton 36, 37, 74, 76, 80, 88, 92
cotton gin 75
crinolines 23, 45

department stores 42, 89, 92
doublet 13, 21, 92
dresses 22–23, 34, 38, 45, 49, 50, 51, 52, 54, 55
dye 12, 36, 60, 89, 92, 93

factories 35, 48, 72–73, 93
fashion designers 11, 33, 36, 38–39, 46, 49, 50, 51, 52, 58, 59, 60, 61, 62, 63, 64, 65, 66, 67
fashion houses 38–39, 40–41, 89
fashion shows 62, 64–65, 82–83
fast fashion 69, 73
footwear 7, 30–1, 61
(see also "shoes")
French Revolution 36–7

gender-fluid 85, 92
gold 12, 13, 14, 88
grunge 65

hats 19, 28-29
haute couture 40–41, 56, 89, 92
helmets 28
hemline 23, 50, 92
high fashion 17, 92
hippies 60
Hollywood 52-53, 78–79

identity 10–11, 17, 28, 84–85, 92, 93
inclusivity 84–85, 92
Indigenous 17, 60, 92
individuality 16–7
Industrial Revolution 35, 36

jeans 25, 65, 82
jewelry 12, 14–15

knickerbockers 16, 24, 92

lace 92
lamé 39, 61, 92
leather 30, 87, 91
linen 20, 74, 88
logos 21, 92
lurex 61, 92
luxury 12, 14, 34, 40, 64, 67, 85, 92, 93
lycra 61, 90, 92

"make do and mend" 54–55
magazines 51, 52, 56, 79, 82, 84, 85, 89
mannequins 55
mantua 34, 92
menswear 34, 44, 50, 57
microplastics 80, 93
mills 36, 93
minimalism 64
mini skirt 58, 59, 91
models 38, 59, 62, 79, 84, 85
movies 52–53, 78–79
museum 6, 66, 74
music 50, 61, 65, 91

national costume 10, 93
nostalgic 60, 78, 93

online marketplaces 68–69

panniers 23
papyrus 30, 93
Paris 34, 38, 40, 48, 51. 56, 89
patent 75, 88, 90, 91, 92, 93
pattern (decorative) 76–77
pattern (dressmaking) 72, 93
pearls 16, 17
petticoats 23, 37, 55, 93
photography 44, 53
polyester 75, 93
punk 61, 91
purple 12, 17, 89
pajama 24

rayon 75
ready-to-wear 42, 59
recycling 81

satin 51, 93
Savile Row 41, 89
S-bend dress 22, 48
secondhand 60, 69, 81
sewing machines 42, 72, 73, 89
silhouette 49, 51, 52, 54, 55, 57, 62, 63, 90, 93
silk 12, 30, 39, 51, 61, 88, 93
shirts 20–21, 65
shirtwaister 21, 22, 93
shoes 9, 15, 30–31, 32, 34, 50
spandex 90, 93
spinning jenny 35, 88, 93
stomacher 37, 93
streetwear 17, 65, 93
suits 34, 44, 50, 54, 62

sumptuary laws 12–13, 88, 93
supermodels 62
sustainability 80–81, 82, 87, 91, 93
sweatshops 72, 93
synthetic 53, 74, 75, 81, 93

tailoring 41, 89, 93
textile 7, 34, 35, 36, 38, 70, 72, 74–77, 92, 93
tie-dye 60, 93
timeline 88-91
traditional dress 14, 17, 28
transgender 85, 93
trends 57, 62, 65, 82–83
pants 24–25, 44, 51, 57, 65
T-shirt 20, 21, 46, 64
tunic 21, 34, 49, 88, 93
turban 28, 54, 93

underwear 21, 48, 53, 57, 63
uniform 48, 54, 93
unisex 82, 85, 93
Utility Clothing 54

velvet 61, 93
Vogue magazine 79, 85, 89

wigs 34
wood 30, 75, 76,
wool 27, 74
World War I 48, 51
World War II 27, 52, 54–55, 56, 57

zips 15, 53, 58, 90

ACKNOWLEDGEMENTS

The authors would like to thank everyone who has helped to make this book, especially the museums, archives, and collections who look after the history of clothing for future generations to discover.

A History of Fashion for Children © 2025 Thames & Hudson Ltd, London
Text © 2025 Celia Joicey and Dennis Nothdruft
Illustrations © 2025 Rose Blake

First published in the United States of America in 2025 by
Thames & Hudson Inc., 500 Fifth Avenue, New York, New York 10110

All Rights Reserved. No part of this publication may be reproduced or transmitted in any form or by any means, electronic, or mechanical, including photocopy, recording, or any other information storage retrieval system, without prior permission in writing from the publisher.

EU Authorized Representative: Interart S.A.R.L.
19 rue Charles Auray, 93500 Pantin, Paris, France
productsafety@thameshudson.co.uk
interart.fr

Library of Congress Control Number 2024932512

ISBN 978-0-500-65336-4
01

Printed in China by C&C Offset Printing Co. Ltd

Be the first to know about our new releases, exclusive content and author events by visiting
thamesandhudson.com
thamesandhudsonusa.com
thamesandhudson.com.au